"A laugh on every page, Christina Ox

western world."

MW01613591

—Robert F. Kennedy Jr.

"Oxenberg's musings on local culture suggests a style that hints of Tom Wolfe,

but with the detached wry and dry observation of Joan Didion, tossed with more

than a splash of charming, classy, self deprecating amusing neurotica that is all

her own."

—Dale Launer *My Cousin Vinny, Dirty Rotten Scoundrels*

"Christina Oxenberg is not only the hottest but also the edgiest writer to emerge

this year. Don't miss the thrill of reading her new book."

—Edward J. Epstein *The Hollywood Economist: The Hidden Financial Reality*

Behind the Movies

"Oxenberg has always scandalized polite society- she is, after all, the daughter of

a royal princess- and has chosen to live in the manner of her writing:

outrageously, ironically, comically at times, but fearlessly brave and above all

true and fresh."

—Taki

"Cynics will want to knock it, considering the pedigree it comes from, but that will be tough because Royal Blue's version of a bad and privileged childhood is funny, fetching, and full of gorgeous writing with a deep, tugging undercurrent of melancholy. Its intimate rendering of wealth without cliché is a triumph–imagine Evelyn Waugh rewriting Eloise. For a first novel, what's most remarkable is that there's not a bum sentence in the entire thing."

–Bret Easton Ellis *American Psycho*

"Oxenberg depicts in exquisite detail the grotesque side of privilege."

–Dominick Dunne *A Season in Purgatory*

"This book will curl your hair, with humor, tragedy and modern despair."

–Eve Babitz *Black Swans*

"This story is full of zest and humor, but the pain borne by the increasingly streetwise heroine permeates every page. I think the book is excellent: very compelling and very well written."

–Hugo Vickers *Cecil Beaton: A Biography*

"Darkly funny."

"Oxenberg shows herself a master at pulling away comfortable, familiar ground...
Oxenberg creates a languid, ferociously beautiful and barbarous world, with an
atmosphere reminiscent of that which pervades the work of F. Scott Fitzgerald..."

"Though Oxenberg insists the book "is not a tell-all," its portrait of a daughter
and her charmingly irresponsible European princess mother echoes Christina's
relationship with Elizabeth, a socialite who counts Prince Charles as her second
cousin..."

Christina Oxenberg

Will Write for Compliments

For Mousca,
from Christina
Oxenberg

with gratitude

Table of Contents

The Key West Series

Also by Christina Oxenberg

Royal Blue

TAXI

And

Do These Gloves

Make My Ass Look Fat?

This book is dedicated to my

Fairy Godmother

Will Write for Compliments

Snapshot

"NOW I'VE GOT YOU," Darren told his wife as they left the church. He felt a huge relief that the wedding was behind them.

It was a breezy summer day in the desert. The young couple, both dressed in white, were walking out of the cool adobe building with a cross on its domed roof. They had invited no guests, only a taxi to take them to the campsite: Darren's idea.

Kristen beamed a giddy smile. She stared lovingly at her husband as they stepped outside into a glaring sun. Inwardly she felt panic. They had been married less than five minutes and the seed of doubt was abloom. She caught the train of her dress in the taxicab door, and like an SOS a lacy white scrap flapped as they drove to the campgrounds.

Later, after they had too much to drink, she begged him to explain his comment. They sat cross-legged on a down-filled mattress under a canvas tent. Darren had thought of everything, including an ice bucket filled with beer.

"Don't get wobbly," Darren commanded, and brandished his beer bottle at her. "Drink to that!"

"Promise not to become normal? Drink to that, too!"

"Promise not to get fat?" he slurred. The surprise in her brown eyes emboldened him, and it was a lucky thing he soon fell back onto the pillows and passed out. In the year of their courtship they had never fought.

The first day of their honeymoon they hiked through a wild canyon. Darren was passionate about taking photographs and relegated gobs of time to this hobby. Hours sometimes passed while he set up his shots. Kristen used this time for daydreaming. One day, long after the dissolution of this first marriage, Kristen would become a writer.

Twenty-four hours since the nuptials they were tramping single file down a crumbly path of dust that hugged the side of the cliff. The scenery was a wide-open canyon of orange and pink stripy rock. The sun was searing and the air smelled of twice-baked heat. There were no handrails, just a sharp drop off to cacti and jagged rock, a deathtrap should a person fall.

Darren snapped pictures. He told Kristen where to stand, how to pose. Next she took the camera from him and began to direct. There was a ledge made from a smooth flat boulder.

"Go stand on that rock," Kristen whispered, immediately nervous. Darren made his way out onto the boulder. Wind blew his thin hair. Through the viewfinder Kristen saw her future.

"Go out a little further," Kristen coaxed, the camera concealing her face. She felt the flutter of guilt.

Carefully Darren inched to the edge and tiny pebbles began noisily trickling over the sides. Possibilities were swirling in Kristen's mind. She was thinking there was sympathy for the widow while none for the divorcee.

They stared at each other, as if for the first time, panting almost.

Faded

SOME TIME AGO IN A FARAWAY PLACE there lived a long-forgotten cabaret singer named Fay. Once famous for her vibrato and her beauty, Fay dwelled in increasing obscurity. According to legend, the interior of her home was said to have every inch of wall hung with framed photographs of herself in her prime. Many of the pictures were autographed by her, and even dated.

On occasion, Fay ventured off to mill amongst the common folks, driven by the hopeless desire to be recognized. There had been a time when paparazzi had mobbed her (after her publicist had clued them in on her coordinates), had blinded her with flashbulbs. But that time was stretching into a mythical past, stretched like her bespoke face and her narrow-lipped, phony smile. One afternoon Fay went for a walk. She had abused the morning bossing her retinue as they gussied and primped her ready for a close-up. Off she sauntered, tripping down the cobblestones that meandered toward the village. When she passed a person, she would swish her head and float her long, red hair around her mean face. She would slyly look from the corner of her eye (which, after so many face-lifts, made her black eyes cross), hoping vainly to catch a glimmer of recognition.

Repeatedly, there was no hint of acknowledgment, and she was ever more crushed. Where had her fans gone? she mused bleakly. Suddenly, while she was deep in thought, she was almost toppled by the gregariousness of a huge brown dog. Furious that the folds of her pretty dress might have been splattered by the heedless hound she swatted at the dog. But the dog was enormous, more like a pony, and her feeble protestations were as inconsequential as a gnat.

While she flailed, the dog bounded excitedly, rising up and planting muddy paws on her chest.

"Stop it!" Fay cried. "Don't you know who I am?"

But the dog misinterpreted her remonstrations and instead found her distress encouraging and he bounced higher and more excitedly.

From nowhere there appeared two young girls slung with cameras. They stopped and observed the scene for a moment and then they approached.

"Photograph? Please?" they said, in broken English.

Fay instantly pulled herself together. The ecstasy she felt spreading from deep within manifest into a widening smirk as she hastily smoothed her dress and fixed her russet hair.

"Of course!" Fay said, addressing the girls. Her heart swelled with confidence, with certainty.

And so the girls began to snap away, taking shot after shot. It took a moment before Fay realized that the girls were photographing the dog. Fay stared in consternation. She took a step backward and then another, almost as if she were testing the improbability of the scenario.

The shock was so devastating, Fay dashed back to her home, and she was never seen again.

White Makes Right

I WENT TO MEET MY FRIEND Elijah at the beach. He was already there when I arrived. I parked and got into his car. It was a warm sultry evening. Elijah had pizza and a beer for each of us. Our plan was to chow and watch the sunset.

Twilight encroached, and I paid no mind to the occasional car pulling up alongside. But then floodlights filled the car.

"Cops," Elijah deduced, frowning at his rearview mirror.

I swiveled around to see three cars pulling in behind us, blue and white lights swirling. The cruisers stopped, a squad of policemen seeped out and strategically surrounded us.

I was perfectly relaxed, faintly amused. I thought for sure they had come to offer assistance: Help us evacuate from a rogue hurricane, or spread news of a visiting serial killer.

"Stay in the car. Keep you hands where I can see them. Don't make any sudden moves." Instructions were reeled off. Were they joking? Right away, things didn't sound right, and I was on edge.

One policeman stuck his head in the driver's side window, and coolly said, "What's up, Elijah? Step out of the car."

Elijah grumbled half-heartedly, which made me all the more uneasy. We both exited the car. I was directed to sit myself down on a split rail fence, my pizza slice sitting on my lap, draining its grease into my jeans. I realized the open beers were a problem but not insurmountable. Surely?

Elijah and this flock of law enforcement gathered behind the car. They were chatting cordially. Things were returning to normal, I thought, and I took a bite of stiffening pizza.

Then the lead policeman asked Elijah to put his hands together behind his back, handcuffed him and locked him up in the back of a patrol car. The many officers then set about taking everything from inside Elijah's car and tossing it to the ground.

I was stunned, to say the least. I feebly voiced an objection but was roundly ignored. The night was turning chilly, and when I asked permission to retrieve a shawl from my car, I was told no.

Elijah told me later that his buddy, the senior cop, told him he found a gun in the car. Elijah knew of plenty of stories where police plant contraband and he told me, he "almost lost his shit."

After a good long while I was free to go. Neither Elijah nor I were written citations for the open containers, just warnings not to do it again. Trembling, I got in my own car. I was glad to leave the company of Elijah and this incomprehensible scene. Elijah set about returning his possessions from all over the parking lot to his car. I drove away tense, alert and terrorized.

Later, when I complained to Elijah about the harshness of the policemen, he said, "It's no big thing. It is what it is." Maybe to him. Did I mention Elijah is black as molasses?

Good Taste

EVER SINCE GRADUATING CULINARY SCHOOL in upstate New York close to 10 years ago, Buck has been employed as a chef. If you ask him, he'll tell you he can do anything and everything there is to do, where things concern food. He'll tell you he enjoys a tasty meal.

Buck grew up on some tropical island where he lived with his parents, a stampede of older brothers, one younger sister and a black dog. He remembers a loving family, he remembers innovative games with friends but most acutely he remembers being hungry.

For a pet Buck kept a rooster he had coddled since it was an egg. He named him Johnny. Johnny looked more like a vulture than your typical rooster, with no feathers on his long, bare, knobby neck.

One day, Buck was idling on the back porch, leaning against a bamboo banister – wood cut down by Buck's father with a machete, then hewn smooth and perfect. Buck's father popped his head out the kitchen window and said, "Fetch me Johnny, Son."

Buck cooed to his pet, calling for him. The rooster, busy crowing on the roof of a shed, hopped down to the sandy earth, chumming up dust.

Buck's father was yelling from the kitchen, telling him to hurry it up. But Buck waited patiently. Buck clucked and clicked, and Johnny stalked confidently across the yard, wings wagging. The child and his pet met at the foot of the steps and climbed them together. Buck opened the kitchen door and clucked some more, ushering the bird inside.

The boy and his bird stepped into the kitchen. Buck saw his mother place a pot of water on the lit stove. The family dog lay in the middle of the room on his side, slapping at flies with his long tail. Buck's father handed him his best machete and instructed him to lay the bird's neck across the butcher's block. Buck could scarcely believe what he was being asked to do. But this was his father, whom he had never disobeyed, and it was unthinkable to question.

"Do it!" his father said.

Buck gathered up his trusting bird and attempted to lay the long neck across the cutting board, where old blood had soaked the wood dark. The rooster sensed something was off and began to resist and flap his wings.

Buck was only nine years old but he was strong. He clamped down around the bird and attempted to pin him. He thought he saw a look of confusion in Johnny's beady eyes. For a fraction Buck hesitated and his thoughts ran amok, and he vowed, if he made sure of nothing else, he'd make sure he never went hungry when he was grown. A quick glimpse of his father's serious face and he snapped to attention and back to his task: a task he had observed adults complete countless times, without fussing, without sentimentality.

His mother stood beside the pot on the stove, where steam bubbled up, her hands tucked under her armpits, as was her habit. The steam began coaxing smells from out of ceiling beams suffused from years of pungent vapors.

"Do it!" his father ordered again.

Focused and using all his force Buck overwhelmed the bird, struggling to hold him still, he spread the long featherless neck across the cutting board and struck it a decisive blow with the machete. Buck watched Johnny's head fly across the room, spurting blood.

The dog lunged for Johnny's head and crunched it to a wet mouthful.

Buck's mother swooped down with well-practiced hands and grabbed at the quills, and in a trice the bird was bare.

"Put Johnny in the pot, Son!" His father said, less loud but just as forcefully.

Buck picked up the corpse and walked to the stove. Stretching on tiptoes, and with the minimum splash, he heaved the bird into the boiling water.

Buck took a step back and swallowed his feelings. He hoped his father would praise him.

A noise like an explosion came from the stove. The heavy iron cooking pot was shuddering. Hissing hot waves shot over the lip, momentarily dousing the flames beneath. Like a bad dream, Johnny's body came out from the cooking pot and flopped to the floor, startling everyone, including the dog, which darted from the room, gripping the rooster's cleaned skull in his jaws.

The twitching bird began to scoot around, slamming against chairs and walls, tumbling in a mess of watery blood and sticky feathers.

"Son, put Johnny back in the pot!" Buck's father commanded.

Buck stumbled after the crashing headless bird until he had recaptured it. Now thoroughly dead, Buck noted the weight of the animal as he hefted it back into the cauldron.

That night, the family ate Johnny along with fried plantains and rum spiked coconut milk. They feasted in silence, except to groan appreciatively at the wondrousness of a proper meal. If you ask him, Buck will tell you he vividly remembers "Johnny tasted good."

Bare with Me

YESTERDAY, EARLY EVENING, I had an hour to fill. Like many of us when faced with downtime, I turned to the Internet. In about a minute I was IM'ing a total stranger. He called himself "Feral Bard".

"What are you wearing?" he typed.

"Nothing," I lied.

We worked up a speedy volley, each outdoing the other for points on wit and originality. Had it been a game show we'd both have won a million dollars. In moments we were naked, so to speak, speaking candidly of desire. The thrust was so direct. I fell in love. I worried the priggish site would evict us for our stripped-bare vulgarities. I hurriedly eyed a clock; 45 minutes remained.

We threw compliments around and flirted like it was our last day on earth. He wanted the camera turned on.

I typed, "No sir."

He told me to send him a photograph. I refused. His begging was thrilling. Perversely, it made me feel high to hold out on him.

He told me he was hard.

I believed him. "I'm sure," I typed.

He sent me his phone number, implored I call.

He wrote, "To hear your voice would be the ultimate eroticism."

I replied, "No sir." I knew it would be the end of things. Why return to reality any sooner than necessary?

"Call me now," he beseeched.

"No!" I wrote. "Fantasy so much better."

I found his insistence and his sternness massively sexy. Yet, as I typed salacious snippets, I was exploding laughing.

The beauty of the chasm the Internet provides is the time to think, to debate, right there in real time and yet utterly in private all at once. I could type one thing, think another and divulge nothing.

"Don't you want to hear me when I come?" He wrote, "Phone me now!"

Suddenly, there were only five minutes before I'd have to log off. I felt I was already deep down the rabbit hole, so why bother with bourgeois convention?

I phoned. I asked him if he had a name. He spoke not one word. All I heard was breath. I tried to coax him, I spoke softly at him, but all I got was labored breathing, heavy, fast puffs of oxygen. I half expected to hear a death rattle, and then the line was cut. I checked my watch. I was late by two minutes.

"Didja?" I typed, as I put on my coat.

"Was better as fantasy," he responded.

Coat on, computer closed, I was in an excellent hyper-jazzed up mood. I would have written back but I didn't have the time.

I had to go. I had a date.

Paved with Good Intentions

EMMA TWIDDLED THE RADIO while I steered her five-year-old diesel Mercedes. It was a habit of ours to fill an evening roving the borough of Manhattan. A favorite pastime was to race the taxicabs.

Emma didn't like to drive and she didn't like to talk and this was fine with me. I preferred to listen to the radio. Apparently her parents never spoke to her – not a word, not at their Main Line Philadelphia dinner table, not ever. But they gave her a brand-new Mercedes for a college graduation present.

One night a cab sliced in front of us to pick up a fare, and we adjusted to pursuit mode, revving up to the bumper when we idled at red lights.

Emma smiled wanly, which meant she was having a rollicking good time. Few people understood Emma, wrote her off as a "little slow." I thought I understood her.

Except for one strange episode when she insisted she had to pee, expressly at a friend's place on the lower East Side. Where Emma met those types I never knew. I didn't like to park the car in that neighborhood but I had a bad feeling about letting Emma out of my sights. I followed her into a tenement building and up a few flights to an apartment devoid of furniture yet carpeted with lounging bodies. Lights were low, music loud, and the place smelled rank from bulk, sodden humanity.

Emma chatted with a man I did not recognize, then crossed the room and closed herself into a tiny toilet. It was a long wait and I got impatient and eventually I went and thumped on the door. It wasn't even locked. It appeared she had been crying. Talking her out of the filthy slum and back into the car was confusingly protracted. It was some time before I understood where we had been.

The cab made to flee westward and I followed close. The passenger swiveled on the back seat, his face troubled.

Emma and I high-fived. When her forearm shot free from the chiffon sleeve, I saw her skin was pocked with welts.

We clattered across West Village cobblestones before the taxi plunged to a halt. The nervy passenger hustled off. But the thrill of the game had dissipated, distracted as I was by my friend's punctured flesh. The limb lay upturned, exposing the terror inflicted near the crook of her elbow. It never occurred to me not to intercede.

After first accusing me of inventing their child's drug use Emma's parents subsequently enrolled her in rehab. Emma escaped but was soon captured and returned. Emma knew I had ratted and never forgave me the treachery. We had not spoken in eons when, years later, I got the news she had died – car crash.

The cabdriver opened his door and surged out, began striding in our direction. He was a grown man and he was in a bad mood.

I swirled around to check exit possibilities and sunk my right foot on the accelerator, backing up down the one-way street, evading the brink.

Outta Sight

OUTSIDE A STORE IN MIDTOWN, I was patting myself with brisk efficiency yet I could not locate my eyeglasses. Amidst a surge of humankind, I stood stock-still and frowned as I tried hard to recall where the heck I might have placed the specs. Adrift in contemplation it was a jolt to hear my name.

I knew the voice, and it snared my attention. I swiveled, and there stood Patrick, a pal of many years. Enthusiastically we embraced.

"Long time! You look fantastic!" Patrick said.

"You look terrific!" I said.

Excitedly we chatted, shared laughs, laughing to the extent we both heaved back and then forward at the same time, braying. This being New York City no one so much as glanced our way.

"Can you tell me what time it is?" Patrick said, and crumpled his shirt cuff to reveal a watch. "I don't have my glasses with me and I can't see a thing."

"Same!" I said, and brandished my own timepiece. "Mine is strictly decorative. My eyesight is so awful I can't even see the hands. Plus, I've lost my glasses. I'm totally blind at the moment."

"Who cares about blindness? So long as we look great!" Patrick laughed. We hugged.

I smiled after him as he melted into the fray, and then I whipped around only to be confronted by my reflection in the store window. Least, I thought it was me. Once again I was frisking myself in pursuit of the missing eyeglasses.

Outta Control

THERE ONCE LIVED a curmudgeonly troll. The troll was not entirely bad-tempered; for example, he responded well to direct sunshine, to the scent of honeysuckle on a warm breeze, or coffee brewing or bacon frying. But this troll was easily irritated and with a stripe of malevolence, he could be a bit lethal. Mostly he kept to himself, and it was better for all that way.

On sunny days the troll enjoyed a stroll. Up hillocks and down dells he ambled distractedly through wild flower prairies. One dawn, interrupting his musings, speeding along came a frog. Green with brown spots, the frog hopped into view, noisily sucking up and spraying dew with the pads of his spindly toes.

The frog came bounding at the troll, startling him.

"Blighted uneducated tadpole!" the troll fumed. And like a spark on gasoline he was engulfed, inflamed with spite, and he very deliberately stuck out a leg, barring the path of the approaching frog.

"I'll school you, frog," he grumbled and he made as if to trip up the frog, and then at the very last moment, as the frog was right up on him, he withdrew his leg.

For his part, the frog saw the troll stick his leg out across the path, and being agile, he adjusted for the obstruction. As the frog and the troll passed each other, their eyes locked. The troll blazed with self-righteousness. The frog was focused on correcting his course. Confounded by this deliberate wickedness he wished he could stop and demand an explanation; but he was late, as it was. Except then he was overcorrecting, his thrust overpowering his speed, so that the amphibian, usually so nimble, began to spin out. The frog could not believe this was happening to him.

From the troll's peripheral vision he thought he saw the frog was wildly out of control, heard the sounds of a sod-spitting skid. The troll hurried away and refused to permit himself to look back. He was feeling twinges of dread as he acknowledged the frog was, potentially, hurt. There were no grounds to believe the worst, he reasoned, as he made wide strides to distance himself from the scene. "Dumb frog might have merely spun around and found himself turned right side up, bounded out of harm's way," the troll muttered aloud, while guiltily, nervously, he scarpered.

His thoughts were consumed with the fate of the frog. He wanted very much to go back and spy on whatever had happened, if anything. But he was afraid and cravenly he locked himself up inside his tree house, turned the lights off and hid.

It would be a long time before the troll could so much as think about the episode without conflagrations of remorse. Adding to his manifesto of homegrown dogma, he etched a commandment that he would never again play a game of chicken, because even when you won, you lost.

On the Loose

LAST SUNDAY when I left Montauk, my plan was simple: I was going to Key West. I didn't know where I'd be staying or how long or any pertinent details, and that was fine by me. All I knew was my destination was a distance of 1,500 miles and would require 24 hours on the road. But I couldn't fully explain my actions so I decided to keep friends in the dark, as they would only pester me for answers I did not have. What if all this manic behavior was a run of the mill midlife crisis? The fewer others I embroiled, the better.

It was midmorning when I skidded out of the parking lot of the Born Free Motel, spraying clamshells. Overnight, from wildest winter, the weather had adopted a sultry humidity tangible in the sunshiny air, and I'll admit it threw me.

Where I had anticipated driving off bloated with smugness, flashing a peace sign to the cold, instead I was questioning everything, like, what in all hell was I doing. And what did any of it have to do with the meaning of life? Anxiety simmered.

The initial stretch on the Long Island Expressway was one I've repeated a trillion times, and any thrill of adventure was tempered by the ho-hum of seeing landmarks I knew by heart. For sport, I gazed into other people's cars, pondering where they were headed, wondering if they could spot the hugeness of my intentions. I didn't have a goat or a sofa strapped to the roof of my car, no telltale signs. I flicked on the heated seats and heated steering wheel and relaxed into the ride.

Somewhere deep in an outer borough, instead of continuing east into the moil of the city I veered south, circumnavigating Manhattan, and for the first time I felt as if the trip had begun. I welled with emotion and a jittery excitement and pressed hard on the accelerator, and before I knew it, I was cresting a bridge, marveling at man's creations and suddenly I was in New Jersey. And there everything came to a screeching halt.

The Turnpike was infested with inching traffic. Exits to gas stations where prices were low, were clogged. The Garden State was excruciatingly slow to cross. Boredom combusted when I could find nothing on the radio, my cache of snacks was depleted, and despite the heated seats, I felt whiplash developing from repeatedly braking to complete stops. The snarl was so bad I contemplated altering course and driving west, if only for the open highway. In an attempt to sop up time and nervous energy, I reached for my telephone. Despite all my positing for remaining covert, my resolve collapsed in the face of stultifying dullness. With reckless abandon I started making phone calls.

TO BE CONTINUED...

On the Loose: Part Two

I HUFFED, inching in traffic as Delaware melded into Maryland – so much for my great escape. This was not the hair-in-the-wind speedy getaway I had envisaged. Five hours in the car so far under a searing sun, with 20 hours to go, I rolled down my window, stuck my head out and yelled, "What kind of drugs was I dosed with when I made this plan?"

Instantly, my phone was ringing, and I reasoned it must be the good Lord enquiring after my ennui. I grabbed for the cell phone and instead sent it flying out of reach. When I returned my attention to the road, I was a millimeter from ramming the trunk of the car ahead of me. Rattled, I exited and pulled into a gas station to fuel up and check my messages. One spam call. I returned to the highway and soon the sun was fading and I had cleared the District of Columbia. Against a backdrop of familiar-sounding cities I crushed the states of Virginia and North Carolina. This was the first time I had driven this route but I had heard of almost every city I passed, and the whole experience felt decidedly safe. "The days of feeling like an explorer are long over," I thought.

It was 2 a.m. as I cruised into South Carolina, and here anything recognizable vanished. I had never heard of a single town mentioned on the signs. The highway appeared to narrow as it cut through a forest, and other than the billboards advertising fireworks, it was just the road and me. I was noticing how dark it was when the sky lit up with lightning and I jumped in my seat. I don't know how it happened but the road split in two and, I think, I took an exit. Suddenly I was lurching and skidding on a dirt track where there were no lights and no signs. And then thunder exploded like a drum section warming up, and down poured a monsoon. Finally GPS returned to life and recalculated my route, and somehow I had 100 miles before I could re-enter the highway. With the gas gauge close to empty I worried and prayed the entire way. Like never before in my life I was wide-awake. At last, I thought, this is the thrill of adventure.

By 4 a.m. I was nearing Savannah, Georgia and I could no longer see straight. My eyes were blurred with floating shapes and I steered to a motel. When I got out of the car, my legs buckled.

A girl, maybe 20, checked me in. With an apologetic grimace, she said, "*Oim* sorry to tell you, but breakfast is served from 6 a.m. to 9 a.m."

I was shocked. "Are you English?" I had to ask.

"*Oim* American, but me parents are British." And then she proceeded to tell me how tourists complain about a stretch of highway apparently possessed by a devil. "Careful what you wish for, is all *oil* say." And she winked.

On the Loose: Part Three

'TWAS MY SECOND DAY on the loose and when I crossed from Georgia into Florida my old pal Beaux telephoned. He too was in Florida. It was so unlikely that we would both be in the same place at the same time we felt obliged to take advantage. Mid-afternoon I parked in Palm Beach and met up with Beaux and his youngest son Max, downing sandwiches and oversized fries at Greene's Pharmacy.

They recounted how, "Right in front of Mummy's house!" they had caught a shark, line casting from the beach. "We stuck poles in the sand and right away we saw fins!" One pole bent from strain, and Beaux reeled a medium-size spinner shark onto the sand, where it went mad. In the chaos one of them suggested, "Grab it by the tail!" And just as someone did, the shark was thrashing back into the surf, where it vanished, dragging the fishing pole away forever.

Leaving Greene's Pharmacy, Beaux asked, "What kind of car you driving?"

Sensing a trap, I settled for vague. "Gray," I replied.

"Can I drive?" he asked, utterly rhetorically.

It transpired Beaux had scheduled a three-hour round trip inland to visit Belle, retired housekeeper, who had worked for the family since before he was born. On the way, Max bleated about how he was "gonna burst!" I winced when Beaux handed back an empty bottle, which Max did his best to fill, and I tried not to picture the inevitable spillage. The pee was pungent so I opened my window. We found Belle in her wheelchair by a window.

"I was your favorite, right?" Beaux asked, and introduced Max for the first time. Belle smiled, and mumbled anecdotes of times long gone. She will turn 103 this June. Max cried when he said goodbye.

Finally we were in the ocean, bodysurfing on the mild froth. I was loving the warm water – until something touched my leg.

"Shark!" I screamed and shot to shore, heartbeat thwacking. Beaux departed to catch a flight, and I stayed at his mother's for dinner. This necessitated a change into my only ladylike dress. After the plates were cleared, we played a word game with tiles and lots of rules, which were vigorously argued over. Beginner's luck – but I won all the games. This went over like a ton of bricks.

I stayed the night in a friend's handsome home on the Intracoastal. Comfortable and spotlessly clean, it was nothing like the motel from the night before.

In the morning, bonding with the luxury, coffee in hand, I stepped onto a balcony and gagged. I snapped, "How did Palm Beach make me her bitch?"

I retrieved my car from the depths of a basement garage of cement and dirty air. Last thing I did before I hit the highway was toss out the bottle of piss. Like a taunting reminder, the spilled pee had reacted with the elements and crystalized, covering the backseat floor mat with silvery flakes, like insect's wings.

And onward and southbound, to Key West, without further delay –

The End

I LIMPED OUT HERE back to the breathable shore and I'm further east than I've ever stayed before. I thought I would pass a fortnight in Manhattan and then continue my journey to Key West. Except I got crumpled from the city sojourn and instead of south I drove as far east as is possible and took a room in Montauk, the very last village on the south fork of Long Island. For one thing, I keenly needed a nap, and my instincts took me home – home in the loosest sense.

I am in a room across the street from the beach and from my porch I can see a slab of the ocean. In between the motels, there is a gap, and I have a peepshow view of the water with its dark spume-flecked waves heaving up to shore. Occasionally the vista is enlivened by a passing pickup truck rattling with fishing poles and coolers. Other than my cigarette smoke, the air is salty and sweet smelling, and the overall effect is invigorating – exactly the palliative I sought.

From the briefest of glimpses, it appears Montauk has a cosmos of its own whirling along, contrariwise to the rest. While the fancy Hamptons to the west are economically beset, here there exists a bustling community. Main Street thrums. The born and bred Montaukers are friendly and possibly all related. In the supermarket the large-boned locals continually called out "hellos" to each other, using first names. Most startling of all was the launderette where I automatically sought out the Latina, who turned out to be a patron (I groveled apologies). Meanwhile, the owners were a mother, son and daughter team sporting an increasingly familiar look of knock-knees, stringy blonde hair and easy smiles.

When I went to pay my bill and extend my stay, I found the motel manager seated in a sagging folding chair, his feet up on a splintering desk and chomping on a large muffin. Atop a hay bale of lank hair, he wore a cap with "The End" stitched across the front.

He asked me if I ever get bored. "I see you spend a lot of time by yourself," he said and rubbed crumbs from a landslide of stubbled chins.

As congenial as the denizens are, I get the feeling they are as pleased to see a tourist come to their town as they are to see one leave.

"Hardly!" I laughed and I could only shrug and smile and scoot back to the sanctity of my quarters from where I can listen to the waves crushing the beach and the screeching bickering gulls. Unlike the nearby cacophonous metropolis, here there are few sounds beyond the surf and the seagulls – except at night when a whipped-up breeze bashes at the windows, pushes on the front door as if it had an invitation. After two weeks in Manhattan I would rather a visit from a gust of wind – and now a long nap, and then it will be time to go.

Carpetbaggin'

A COUPLE YEARS AGO I stayed in this motel in the village of Southampton, and here I am again. I recognize the receptionist, which is a trifle shocking since in the interim I feel I have lived several life spans. I will spend one night here and hit the highway in the morrow for a spate in Manhattan in the guest room of a pal – then onward, destination TBD.

I am moving again. A rented storage space is crammed full, my car is laden, and I am on my way. The only difference with this move is that while I knew that I was leaving Southampton and I even knew specifically when I was to depart, I have yet to figure out where I'm headed.

Friends keep asking me where I'm going, which is annoying, since I have no clue, and frankly I don't see why they need to know unless they plan on sending cards or gifts, which I might add, they never do. So why do they pester? Why do they gotta know? Much more worthwhile would be if one of them could tell me where I'm going, unless it is to hell, in which case they can keep the news to themselves.

Here are some of my choices: (comparable cost-wise)

Airy bungalow in Key West

Hovel in Brooklyn

Hmm, hovel in Brooklyn is really popping out, luridly. Every time I imagine life in a grotty urban apartment, I flashback and shudder. In between the occasional loaned, lavish spread, I have stumbled into some unutterable hovels – places to lie on the floor in a stupor of disbelief.

One time when I got myself in the crosshairs of Karma, through the friend of a friend I rented a studio in Greenwich Village for five hundred bucks a month. It was so cheap I felt compelled to take it. Not only was I robbed by the neighbors from downstairs; I was also flooded from upstairs, which resulted in a mushroom crop sprouting right out of the trammeled leopard-print carpet. The experience was so dispiriting I booked a one-way ticket to Belize and traipsed around Central America for several months. The further south I explored, the more I fixated on visiting the Galapagos Islands, and I almost did, except I ran out of money in Guayaquil, Ecuador. But that is entirely another story.

Which reminds me why I am carpetbagging: It is time for an adventure, plus my lease was up. All I know for certain is it is most definitely time for an unalloyed lark.

At least I hope so. I'm really not sure. Knowing the unplumbable depths of my perversions, I won't be too surprised if I never cross the state line and instead plant my flag in an outer borough.

Whirl Girl

I STORMED INTO THE BANK, on a mission. I am moving and I have very little time to squander. With me I had my tiny green paper envelope which contained the special key for the lock box. I accosted the first bank employee I came across – female, young, unfriendly. She was useless. Couldn't get anything to work right.

I grumbled about incompetence.

A man came along and tried to intervene. He fumbled and dropped the keys.

I had some scathing utterances for him, too.

I was bristlingly out of patience.

Then they were telling me the envelopes for their bank keys are red, not green.

I was in the wrong bank.

They united in a front and crossed their arms, smirks spreading.

I mumbled an apology and swallowed down hard on some humble pie.

The walk to the front door felt like a million miles.

To Be Continued

LEO AND I GOT INTO AN ARGUMENT the morning he left for the motorbike competition. It was the last time, as far as I was concerned. I planned on breaking it off with him when he got back.

Right away I felt a massive relief. I was turning over that leaf after weeks of dithering. I could hardly wait to launch the new phase. And then I received a phone call.

A man I did not know was shrieking and frantic. "You need to go to Dover Hospital!" the man was screaming in a blur of static. I did not need it explained that this could only be about Leo.

I was not impressed. I sighed audibly and mumbled, "He better be half dead." I hung up.

Driving the forty minutes to Dover Hospital I fumed and pictured Leo in a wheelchair doing wheelies up and down some ward corridor, driving everyone nuts and me having to waste time on a twisted ankle or some such nonsense.

I was feeling wholly uncharitable. I was doubly annoyed because I was unsure if this turn of events would interfere with my decision to dump him, and triply annoyed with having to waste more time on him with this ridiculous trip to the hospital. As I drove I murmured, "He better be dying."

Glowering at everyone and swaggering with chilly disdain, I badgered nurses until they escorted me to Leo. I was led into a huge room filled with cots, and him on one, propped up with pillows and smiling cheerily. I was getting ready to strangle him when I saw the demolished foot.

The sight stopped me short, like a hand to my chest. His left leg was out from the sheet, and the end of it, where the foot was supposed to be, was what looked like a heap of raw hamburger meat with a huge french fry sticking out of the middle of it. When it became clear that the raw hamburger meat was what was left of his flesh and the french fry was a bone, I pitched forward and vomited, and then I fainted

Wassat?

ACCORDING TO THE TUTORIAL I downloaded, here's how to learn a foreign language:

a) Learn how to say "hi" and "goodbye."

b) Learn how to say "what?"

c) Don't be afraid of looking ridiculous.

Matas Todos (Kill Everything)

THE DRIVEWAY TO MY HOUSE is narrow, encroached upon on three sides by overhanging trees and bordered with bulbous shrubs with holly-like leaves intermingled with orange balls. When I first saw this driveway I loved it on sight. It was so obviously the path to something exceptional. And sure enough, concealed beyond the flora was a cottage with perfection written all over it.

For close to a year I have been exceedingly happy here. But then I bought a new car and my world changed forever.

I used to love birds. I used to swoon at the festoon of Nature's bounty. Now I detest the birds for their emissions which land with suspicious accuracy on the driver's side door handle. Formerly peaceable, today I contemplate the steps required to obtain a gun. Suddenly I loathe trees and shrubs and anything else that might apply unctuous sticky missiles to my vehicular love. Those blasted bushes that line the driveway spatter the machine's immaculate paint job with their gluey orange balls, orange balls that I have come to believe have no earthly reason to exist. Like a person sprung loose from a midlife crisis, I'm thoroughly over the cuteness factor.

Except where cuteness pertains to the car – here I am agog. Recently I took it to the car wash, followed this up with a soft towel and me in the sunshine buffing the sides, wiping away imperceptible traces. I have frequently eyeballed bipeds in driveways of their own, bucket and sponge at hand, lovingly cleaning their cars and secretly I cackled with derision at their petty bourgeoisies. To my eye nothing has ever embodied the concept of bourgeois more than a person pampering a freakin' car. Unasked, I have joined the ranks. Well, I remind myself, this is not the first time I have been wrong.

Next, all I have to do is phone the gardener and ask him to remove Nature from within 10 feet of my car. "Mata todos, por favor," I practice before I telephone. "Kill everything."

Skill Sets

OVERNIGHT, as per predictions, a foot of powder had fallen, reconfiguring my surroundings to a Whistler. When first alerted to the impending blizzard I had every intention of buying a shovel, but a good book got in the way.

Late into the day snow continued to fall so I tore myself from the excellent read. Scuffling with the elements I burrowed a route to my car. I drove to town to find it unrecognizable in its desolation except for a cardboard Santa and his caravan swinging ridiculously in the air over Main Street.

I slid around with the radio playing something classical and I was charmed by the romantic melancholy of it all. Snowflakes continually descended, absorbing noise and obscuring sight. Eventually I had to acknowledge the slide beneath my tires. Carefully, I steered homebound.

There were no tracks on the road to my house, not even those of a plow – no signs of life at all other than a hunchbacked man trudging down my street. At first I figured he must be deranged, as this was not strolling weather. On approach, I saw he was wearing a backpack and carrying something like a broom; closer still, I saw it was a shovel.

Oh, right, a shovel. I meant to buy a shovel. I considered returning to the village. Instead I slowed beside the man and asked him if he was looking for work.

"Si," he told me, and we struck up a deal. His name is Victor and for the rest of the winter Victor will be my shoveler. Thank the heavens; I'm now returned to reading. Long live Victor.

In with the New

JANUARY, SUNDAY, and the East End was unnaturally balmy. A cloud reclined on the ground, spreading itself generously in amongst denuded shrubbery, smudging outlines. For an instant the sun burned a hole through the heavy gray haze.

Enthused by the splash of daylight I ventured out for a drive. Dirty ice and slick mud lined long residential streets. Overlooking the beach, from behind high dunes where snow obstinately clung, I watched a girl on a pecan brown pony. There was something in the way she held the reins, her arms wide and stiff, as if she was unfamiliar with horseback riding. Despite the distance, I could see she was smiling.

It was early afternoon and I continued on my survey. Houses appeared to slumber, shut up with curtains and blinds drawn. They did not look derelict; rather they seemed bloated and suspended, somehow, as if in the middle of a yawn. Tubs and crates had been dragged to the end of driveways, near the curb. Plastic bins stuffed with folded cardboard and red and green wrapping paper and spilling over with strings of ribbon skittering on the breeze.

Soon the remnants of the recent past will be trucked away, and we will catch a collective breath and forge ahead with this New Year.

Happy New Year.

Happy Holidays

DECEMBER, NEW YORK CITY, it was twilight and I was strolling southbound on Madison Avenue.

A truck and a crew were working over a steaming hole in the middle of the slimy avenue, their section marked off with portable bollards that would do little more than mark the spot should an accident occur.

From the hole emerged a man in overalls with yellow reflective tape in a grid on his torso. He was looking my way, though not at me. He looked purposeful. After waiting on a cab to pass, the man closed the distance to the sidewalk in a few strides. He strode directly to a shop window and stopped in front of it, a men's watch store.

Cruising past the wall of black glass, I caught an eyeful of dark velvet topped podiums, each with a single outrageous timepiece illumined by spotlights. The city employee paused at the vitrine, his eyes bulging in their sockets. While the mass of him came to a halt, his mind clearly went wild.

Or so it seemed to me as I ambled slowly by. I knew it was the right thing to do, to leave him alone in his altered state of nirvana, but I couldn't resist, and so I doubled back and paused beside him. In the reflection of the window I watched his face, followed his eyes roving across the goodies.

"You have a watch fetish," I volunteered.

The man stared straight ahead and said nothing to me. I thought I detected his craggy cheek twitch.

"It's OK," I told him to encourage him to relax, "I have a watch fetish too. It happens." And I asked him which one was his favorite.

For a moment of true worship in silence we marveled at the extreme bling. I can't say I know where the man's thoughts traveled. For me, I saw flashes of Omar Sharif slash Puff slash white tails.

After careful consideration he said, "That one," pointing at a spectacular creation entirely encrusted with crushed diamonds. It was mighty handsome. He added, "Although it's kind of ostentatious."

Never taking our eyes from the prize, side-by-side we absorbed the loveliness and smiled, tacitly acknowledging the charm of fantasy is never having to explain oneself.

Invigorated by the whiff of daydream snuff, we wished each other some happy holidays.

Ketchum, if You Can

I JUST SPENT A FEW DAYS in the Rockies of Idaho, in a snow-globe, deep-freeze, sun-drenched valley thousands of feet above sea level. I had been asked to read from my new book by the Ketchum Community Library.

This came to pass because Sabina Dana Plasse, currently arts and events editor of the Idaho Mountain Express, brought my book to the powers that be at the library, and they extended an invitation. My ego was tickled pink and I accepted. Ever since, for the past couple months, I have lived suspended in a state of excitement and terror.

Dana and I met 10 years ago when we were both struggling. We wanted to be writers but met mostly with obstacles, and legions of naysayers. We lost touch and now – a decade later and thanks to the possibilities of social networking – we have reconnected.

The town of Ketchum is fairy-tale Cowboy. My second day I did the reading at the very magnificent five-star-hotel/ski-lodge of a library with a roaring fire and cathedral ceilings of sultry, dark beams. As if by some extraordinary tumble into another dimension, I watched myself striding toward a podium in front of a roomful of seated, expectant, complete strangers. I looked at the faces looking right at me and I figured I must be dreaming because I would never have the guts to do such a thing as this.

Instead of freezing, as I'd expected, I got totally carried away and told stories and chatted on and on, and then when I realized I must have abused a good chunk of time, I said, "OK, that's probably enough about me – if anyone has any questions?"

No one said anything. All these faces stared at me, no one uttering a word. And then it dawned on me: I had forgotten to read from my book. I asked if I should, and someone called out, "Yes, read a story!" So I did, and then the forgiving and tolerant audience effervesced with questions, and all of us were soon sharing some laughs.

After the library, a group of us stopped in at a restaurant and then wound down at Grumpy's, a bar as tiny as a train carriage and eccentric like a carnival barker's caravan.

I'll be happy for an excuse to go back. I say Ketchum, if you can.

GWON

RADIO JOCKEY: Today our show is honoring the English language. I invite all listeners to phone in and tell me obscure words.

Hello, caller, you're on the air.

Caller: I got a word for you.

Radio Jockey: Terrific. What's your word, caller?

Caller: My word is "gwon."

Radio Jockey: "Gwon." Excellent. I've never that word before. How do you spell it?

Caller: G-W-O-N.

Radio Jockey: Brilliant. And can you use it in a sentence for me, caller?

Caller: "Gwon" fuck yourself. This is the worst radio program I've ever heard.

Radio Jockey: Sorry, listeners. Our calls are not screened. We have another call.

Hello, caller, you're on the air. What's your word?

Caller: "Shmee."

Radio Jockey: "Shmee." That's a good word. Please spell it.

Caller: S-H-M-E-E.

Radio Jockey: Thank you, caller. And can you use the word in a sentence for me?

Caller: "Shmee" again. "Gwon" fuck yourself.

Creative Nonfiction

IT WAS BOUND TO HAPPEN – just a matter of time really, when I sent a raunchy story to the wrong email address. My dirty tale was delivered to the inbox of Rat, this guy I know.

Immediately, Rat wrote back. He typed me about five messages in quick succession. I stared at the monitor and wondered what to do with this commotion I had stirred up. From his tone, it seemed Rat was a happy man. He sounded like he thought he had met his soul mate. Not only didn't he know the story was not meant for him; he also didn't know it was just a story, unadulterated creative nonfiction.

Ever since then, Rat phones and sends me electronic messages, often at four o'clock in the morning. He pleads with me to contact him. I'll probably never call him. I'll certainly never tell him I did a Cyrano de Bergerac to myself.

Rat thinks I'm the coolest chick who ever lived. I prefer to leave him with that impression.

Faux Pas

THE INVITATION OF THE SUMMER arrived in my inbox. It was a glittering option. If I was ever going to show up, this ought to be that time. Given the choice I would never leave home because I get so twisted up. My only banter for weeks on end is answering rhetorical questions posed by TV shows.

But now and again I feel I have to put in an appearance, crippling social phobias be damned. At the last moment I chose a particular pair of shoes, very high and perilously unsteady.

I stressed beforehand. I stressed traveling there. I took winding back roads, the back roads to the back roads. Obviously, I was going out of my way to never reach the fancy party. Truth was I was terrified.

One guest called me a minx, but my high anxiety translated this to manx. "I love cats," I said, starting to relax.

"I said minx," the man reiterated.

"You're calling me a ferret?"

"Not minks, minx."

It wasn't a strong moment. With another interlocutor I had to confess I had never heard of the author he referenced. He was horrified by my ignorance. I might as well have admitted to high crimes.

Worst was when I told a world-famous writer I was currently reading his book. When he asked me which one of his books I was reading, I blanked on the name. Terror. A few words popped into mind and I chucked them out. It was a good try, but I got the tittle wrong. The author turned his attention away. And these were just the highlights.

My faux pas carbon footprint was effectively used up, and it was time to go. Gratefully, I made for the exit. I was comforting myself with the notion that I would not have to leave home again for a long time.

I almost reached the front door when, from nowhere, a breeze collected the edge of a carpet. The fringed fabric ensnared the heel of one shoe, and I began to wobble, arms flailing and wheeling and grabbing at air.

By some miracle I did not crash to the ground, only lurched and lunged. I got to the front door and stepped out into the sunshine.

Ho Baby

POKING THROUGH SOME FAMILY treasures I came across a silver photograph frame with Helen Oxenberg engraved, bottom center. The frame is decorated with dainty renditions of rattles, teddy bears, a bow. There is no photograph in the frame.

At close range, I see that below the name, carved in sharp as glass is my birthday. I stared a good, long while at the passive shiny object and waited for a hint. And then just as I was ready to lob it back into a cardboard box, a distant bell trilled, and I remembered a story:

Way back when I was born, 'twas a snowy stormy night in New York City. On the Upper East Side in Doctor's Hospital my mother remembers it was a long delivery. When I finally appeared, Momma was exhausted and in no mood for small talk. She says she only vaguely remembers the nurse asking her for her baby's name. One way or another the name, "Helen" was inked onto my birth certificate.

But then my name was changed, and the episode dissolved into family lore. Here in my hands sits the tiny silver tablet to prove the legend was true: My name is Helen. And this is funny to me because I have always thought Helen was short for "hell in a hand-basket."

Slingin'

DAMIAN IS A DRUG DEALER in present-day New York City. I chauffeured him one afternoon. He settled himself in my car and was careful to buckle his seat belt. Recommending I do the same, he tells me, "That's why the cops will pull you over: something simple like a seatbelt."

Damian is fifty-ish and gray and rumpled and a shopping cart away from looking homeless. He wears a messenger bag with the strap across his chest like a pageant sash. He says he is an alcoholic, though not so much into drugs, because he finds them boring.

He received a phone call: "Hello, Karen, you home? Twenty minutes?" Damian snapped the phone closed and turned to me. "Midtown, please.

93

"I got into this business because I don't need a green card or a resume or people skills, and there's always work. This trade is unaffected by the economy. The only time we get hit is if we have bad shit for too many weeks in a row. When we get complaints we offer full refunds. You never want to lose a customer.

"You're only seeing the mundane side of my job: the traveling around town. Usually I'm in the back of a cab. I pass the time observing humanity. I observe but I stay mum. You can't say anything to anyone here. One time when a pretty girl walked by I did yum-yum noises at her. She turned and looked like she was thinking about phoning the police. I said, 'Oh, I'm sorry. 'Yum-yum' means 'fat and ugly' in your language."

Damian's phone rang.

"Hello. Yes. Hi-Tec? Not today. Sorry, mate. Call me tomorrow." Damian shut his phone. "Focking moron."

"Safety measures include you never take a train or a bus. The greatest hazard of my job is the boss, John. He's a smart guy but he smokes too much and he's losing his shit. For one thing, he likes for me to meet him in restaurants, not suspicious at all, walking into a restaurant and sitting down with him.

"No, thanks. I'll just chew on a breadstick.

"I hand him a stack of cash, and in return he gives me a bulging plastic bag, not a bit suspicious. One time, I was leaving the restaurant, when a waiter tapped me on the elbow. I look down to see I'd dropped a trail of baggies.

"'Pick those up. No one has noticed yet. Pick them up and get out of here' – the waiter was hurrying me!'

"I'm uncomfortable when I go to someone's home for the first time. So I figure the customer must be uncomfortable, too. Why wouldn't they be? They'll say, 'Do you know Tony?'

"And I say yes, and I see that makes them feel better. But I'm already in their home. I'm thinking, 'What if I said, *no, I don't know Tony and now I want you to give me all your valuables?*'

"My second day on the job I answered a call – some guy in midtown. I got to the building, and it looked OK, doorman and everything. I rode the elevator, and as I got to the front door of the apartment, before I even knocked, it swung open. In I went, directly into a fancy hall. Through an open door I could see a huge, naked, bald man playing with himself and staring at a television. I did a double take, and sure enough he's watching a porno movie of a huge, naked, bald man having sex with a blow-up doll. Behind me I heard a cough and I spun around to see a wee tadpole of a man. He was naked and bald. Under other circumstances, I might have said, 'Do us a favor, mate, and put that away.' Instead I was telling myself to stay professional. I'm thinking, 'What the hell am

95

I doing? I'm in someone's apartment with who knows how many more naked, bald fellows on the premises.' But then I snapped out of it, and he paid for his gram of cocaine, and I was out of there."

Damian's phone rang again. "Karen, I'm downstairs. I'll be right up." He closed his phone and got out of my car.

"Thanks for the rides. I'm gonna need a drink after this."

Jaws

AFTER ROASTING ON THE BEACH all afternoon, I wanted to go for a swim. It was late in the day at a Long Island bay, and I flip-flopped to the edge of the surf.

The horizon was wide as a yawn, and the wrinkling waves twinkled. I would have dived in, except there was a flotilla of jellyfish, clear and purple and domed like paperweights. Some hung in the tumbling breakers, others were clustered drying dying on the sand. My desire to swim diminished.

I scarcely noticed the seagull clearing a landing nearby, except the bird seemed bothered and two-stepped a U-turn to evade me.

"Don't flatter yourself, Bird, " I thought. "I'm not interested in you." But then a ruckus in the froth caught my eye.

Marshaling my attention was a child's toy shark, gray and white with a profusion of delicate fins. I considered picking it up, maybe even keeping it. Who would I prank? I planted my feet deep for ballast and stared intently at the plastic item that had rolled over, exposing a whitish, striated tummy. Making my eyes bulge I thought I saw the little mouth open. And then it did it again. The object was panting.

I experienced a moment where I knew my purpose on this earth: I had to save the creature. With the tip of one shoe, I shoved the baby shark into deeper water. But it was on its back lolling uselessly, black button eyes staring heavenward.

Interrupting my communion was the piercing squawks of the seagull. I turned to see him pacing maniacally with his wings half extended so he looked as if he had his hands on his hips. I finally figured out I had grossly interfered with the bird's dinner.

My charitable instincts receded. No need to interfere with nature, I decided and I backed off.

Taken for a Ride

HAVING LIVED in New York City for several years, it has come to my

attention that there is a great deal lacking in the public transportation system. The

first thing that comes to mind is the lack of the cleanliness. There was a time

when I had a job on Wall Street, which necessitated two long subway rides a day.

Each day I had to mentally prepare myself for the intolerable stench, the ever-

growing piles of refuse and general decay of stations. The graffiti that so many

complain about was a welcome distraction from my fellow passengers. Aside

from aesthetics, the commotion of the train was enough to render one quite ill by the end of the journey. The only conceivable attraction to this grizzly experience was the fare – then only 70 cents.

After I quit my job, I vowed never to enter the gray and grimy subway again and turned my attention to the bus. The bus had always appeared as a large and friendly convenience that, for the same price as the subway, promised comfort and safety. Not so. The only comfort was the knowledge that I was no longer on the loathsome subway. As for safety, well, it all depends on the power of your grip as the bus crashes in and out of potholes and then slams on the brakes at the lights.

The rules of the buses are simple. Never take a bus if you have anything less than an hour to waste. Never take a bus if you are tired and need to sit down, as invariably all the seats are covered with truants guzzling down poisonous-looking hot dogs, or ancient women surrounded by hundreds of bags, mumbling obscenities to themselves. And lastly never take a bus for the scenic route as – if you are standing up, which of course you will be – all you will see are the Spanish advertisements placed at eye level.

Finally, I graduated to taxis, not because my standard of living had improved so much but because I had been contracted to write a book about them. Every cab I took was a potential interview, but there were other times when I actually needed to get somewhere fast. The strange irony of New York City taxis is that when you are in a rush, you get the one-eyed lazybones who believes in napping at every red light. And perversely, when you have all day and want to chat, you land yourself the frustrated Formula driver who specializes in careering down the avenues at lighting speed and plastering you to the back seat with mach force to the power of 10.

I believe that the speed-freaks outnumber the dawdlers by 3-to-1. What they all have in common is their complete ignorance of the city's streets.

The only true, reliable form of transportation is to strap a Hoppicopter onto your back and jump out of a window.

Odds Are

KATIE JO was shocked. After less than a year of marriage, her husband was leaving her.

"Feels like I've ruined my life," he declared, flinging items into suitcases. "Like when I went to Penn State instead of holding out for the Ivy League."

In retrospect it was obvious there had been signs of fracture, but Katie Jo had noticed none. She thought they were blissfully happy. Now alone, the shock morphed into catatonic depression, and pals became concerned.

One friend intervened and suggested she attend an Alcoholics Anonymous meeting. "It's a great place to meet new people," the friend counseled. "Everybody there is wounded, like you. They'll be sympathetic."

"But I don't drink!" Katie Jo replied, and then tears welled, and she exploded sobbing. "That was one of his complaints. He said I'm no fun because I don't drink."

"No one will know," the friend urged. "Besides, you don't have to speak at the meeting."

On automatic, Katie Jo looked up information for the nearest meeting. One was listed as "women only," and she decided that seemed like a wise idea. After showering and dressing there was still a half hour to fill, and Katie Jo began anxiously to pace around. On a whim, she checked the fridge. Sure enough, there remained some beers. "If I'm going to hang out with alcoholics, I might as well be crocked," she snickered.

Due to zero tolerance for stimulants and after almost the entire bottle of beer, Katie Jo was plastered. With a thick head and slowed motions, she descended the steps to the street. The sluggish sensation was not unappealing, and when she stumbled down a step and fell clutching at the banister, it was not frightening; instead she was laughing, and spittle flecked her cheek.

The meeting was in the basement of a church – a deep, wide room with an oval wood table and chairs all around, already filled with an earnest-looking congregation. Faces turned to look at her as she took a seat – smiles, discreet nods.

Around the table, they went introducing themselves and their predicament. One woman claimed she was "a slave to chardonnay."

Another said that at her worst with cocaine addiction she had moved in with her dealer.

Then it was Katie Jo's turn. "Hello" – this came out phlegmy, so she cleared her throat and recommenced – "I'm Katie Jo and I would like to become an alcoholic."

All faces were now fixed on her, none of them smiling. The group leader, a portly lady with short, gray hair and round glasses, shoved her chair back from the table and stood up. "Welcome, Katie Jo. Are you trying to be funny?"

"My *huthband* left me," Katie Jo barged on, emboldened. "He *thaid* I am no fun because I don't drink. I figured I'd *athk* the professionals for *tipth*."

All these serious faces stared at her, mouths pursed rigidly. One woman, hugely fat in an orange dress, said, "Have you considered gambling?"

Happy Fourth

EVERY DAY IN KEY WEST at sunset, many gather along the pier to watch the Technicolor-ed sky, along with vendors and performance artists and jugglers tossing flaming sticks. A favorite act is a man who sits perched on an upturned tub, his knees pressed together, all of him curled small. He is concealed behind two enormous palm fronds, which he holds steady. He wears a green velvet pirate outfit and a black tricorn hat over a wild shaggy wig. He sits very still, so that he becomes invisible. He waits until the perfect combination of distracted types approach. Then he strikes, lunging up and forward. Standing tall, he rattles the palm fronds. The passersby scream, and clutch their throats, and grab the hands of their children and pull them close. While the rest of the crowd, us who are in on the joke, cackle with laughter. Only then do the terrified tourists begin to giggle, embarrassed and relieved with eyes wide from misfired fear.

When the sun slides westward the sky becomes a bustle of blues. I paused to admire a salsa band of middle-aged men holding acoustic guitars high up on the crest of swollen stomachs, strumming fast, all of them grinning, eyes closed. In front of the stage an older couple danced – him in shorts and a floral shirt, his lady in flip-flops and fringed sundress. They are facing each other, linked by their fingertips'. Still holding hands, they swing their hips and they twirl around. Synched with the rhythm, they are now side by side, shimmying faster. As one they bend at the knee and scoop to the right and then to the left. They are smiling.

As the sky darkened, the collective mood revved up, energy palpable. In a bar, as I waited on a drink, the musician on stage finished his song and proposed a drinking competition. The first up was a girl, feminine and slim. Her arms were bare, her dress long. She glugged the pint in three seconds and then daintily dabbed at the sides of her mouth with the hem of her dress. Next went a stringy man who dribbled half his drink down his chin in three and a half seconds. He was booed off the stage, and the crowd became agitated. And then a fat man volunteered. His round, florid face was set with a big smile as he accepted the filled glass of amber liquid. He spread his legs in a golfer's stance, waggling his limbs in preparation, and then he swallowed the ale in two seconds flat. The room almost split open from the applause. The seasoned guitar player resumed the entertainment with "Sweet Caroline," and the audience, now raucous, howled the refrain.

In yet another bar, a clutch of hairy musicians played "Mustang Sally." For his solo, the lead used his half-full beer bottle for a fret. When he finished the song, he guzzled the beer. "Drink up," he said. "Happy Fourth of July."

The Key West Series

Breasts

NEAR A PICNIC TABLE four girls slept on the beach. Humps of hips and elbows slashed across faces, blocking out the late afternoon sun. They were zebra-striped with their bands of colors from their bathing suits.

A couple blocks away, a squabbling couple exited a squat bungalow. They bustled into a maroon minivan.

"Victor!" Kay was sobbing. "I can't take it!"

"Please calm down." Victor said, buckling himself, sitting as close to the door as possible. "You shouldn't drive when you're upset. Please let me drive?"

"I'm always upset!" Kay said and shoved a pair of sunglasses onto her swollen, tear-stained face. She rolled down her window, took exaggerated gasps of air.

The maroon van bounced, and the shocks screeched before vanishing around a corner.

The sun was transmuting to the fattened glows of a sunset. A cell phone blared from a bag beside one of the slumbering girls, the shrill sound infiltrating her dreams. In seismic waves, the girls shook awake, shuddering and stretching, still laying on the sandy ground and pulling their arms straight and tight over their heads.

"Victor! Are you listening?" Kay was driving fast. "How many times do I have to tell you? I need affection. I need romance. I need you to take me dancing."

"That's nice," said Victor, distractedly, the edges of his mouth turned down. He was resignedly staring straight out in front. His wife's barrage was muted to fuzz inside his head.

Discordant as unfurling petals, the girls gradually sat up. They were blinking and yawning. One of the girls wore no top. She was wearing nothing but a white bikini bottom. Suddenly dominating the scenery were her firm, high breasts, grapefruit-sized, gravity-defying conicals with small, brown nipples. She stood up and flung out her arms, her hands in fists, then lifting them in wide arcs and making points of her fingertips. She shook out her tangled blonde hair, and the rubbery breasts moved. She arched her back. She knew she was awesome and she was enjoying every moment of it.

"You never listen to me!" Kay exploded, and steered the minivan into the parking lot up to the picnic table, where they liked to sit. Victor had a perfect clear view of the magnificent breasts on the young woman now slowly lowering her arms, all of her moving just enough so that the breasts wobbled.

"Wow!" said Victor, before he could stop himself.

Kay's attention was engrossed with stomping on the brakes and sliding the gears into park, but the tone of her husband's voice caught her in the solar plexus.

"What...?" Kay said and plucked off her sunglasses, glanced quickly at him. Following his cemented gaze she turned her head and examined the scene of the four girls standing just beyond the picnic table. Gradually, the details of the half-naked girl registered, and Kay began to frown.

For the first time in a long time Victor smiled.

Stepping In

I WANDERED BACK toward the new digs -- down along the main street spilling with people visiting the many bars, sucked in by the sounds of music. In a bar played a band, a father and his two sons – him on electric guitar, the older boy with a sleepy eye strumming a silver tape-patched banjo; and the other, lupine, dominating a double bass taller than himself. There was something in the scruffiness of their hair, the blandness of their not-new clothes that suggested swamps. Each had their eyes on the others' hands. Their comfortable trinity hinted at the hours they have rehearsed, honing that groove. They were performing Eric Clapton's "Lay Down Sally" and they infused it with Bayou and fast-paced precision jamming. They were meshing. The three of them – with their serious, far-away countenances, they were coasting as one. Their music was gorgeous, and I could not walk away, first leaning against a tree and staring through the open doorway, then stepping inside.

Iguana Boogie

FROM THE PORCH of my new home, in a rickety chair, I look upon an enchanted view: a garden of rubbery plants and palm trees swaying in a flower scented breeze. The swimming pool is surrounded with white marble, and behind it, a path of coral leads to a short wall, the beach and the ocean. Slim, speedy geckos zip around the swimming pool. A female rushes about in a feverish way and then she stops and slyly looks behind. A beat later, the male peeks from the jungle foliage, where he flares an impressive blood-red wattle. She makes as if to flee, and he chases her like crazy and leaps upon her and pins her for quite some time.

On the swath of blue and green ocean, people aboard all manner of conveyances stir up wakes. Men and their dogs slosh through ankle-deep sand banks. Paddle boarders punt, spooning along. Military fighter jets clatter through the sky, far ahead of the noise they create. Prop planes pass, pulling banners with the paid-for message of the day.

Staring at the ocean, I saw dark shapes pushing through the surface, creating whitewater splashes before melting tracelessly away. Most likely most of these were optical illusions. I contemplated swimming, and I shuddered.

Close to midnight, I went out and walked the main drag, a flash point for all things entertainment. Drunk girls danced by themselves in the street, undulating with their arms in the air, sometimes singing, eyes closed. Cigar smoke insinuated from a couple, arm in arm – him in pinstripes and her in Wild West brothel get-up with enormous breasts spilling from a frilly edged shirt. As they passed, the woman raised a half-smoked cigar to her mouth and puffed like a coal train.

Was nearly knocked down by a wobbly passerby – instead we went for drinks, where I met his friends – lots of laughs.

Suddenly, it was 4:00 in the morning, and I had to force myself to leave. Night and day the heat here is steamy. I was sticky and wanted to go for a swim. When I got home, I disrobed and stepped into the cool pool. Moonlight brightened the night. I dunked all of me, going under several times, and then emerged and bobbed with only my snout out. And then I heard a tremendous

rustling. The underbrush crackled, and I froze.

Shockingly, into the light strode a fat-bellied, long-clawed, lime-green

iguana. He was maybe three feet from flicking tongue to the tip of his black-

ringed tail. As quietly as possible, I pushed to the deep end. The lizard stopped

and scanned for dangers. From the moonlight, I could see his slimy eyeballs

swiveling around. With exaggerated movements, he neared the shallow end. I

held my breath. The little dragon eased his torso over the side and planted his

front feet on the top step. He dipped his face and sipped a large gulp, then tipped

back his horned head, allowing the drink down. Then he hoisted himself out and

slowly dragged himself back into the jungle.

Zdravo Marko

FOR AGES NOW, I have wanted to learn Serbian. Strike that, I have wanted to speak Serbian. The "learning" part has been the obstacle. I intend to visit the country but first I want to learn the lingo. I had hoped something easy would present itself; perhaps I might meet a Serb who could teach me. But instead I was moving, packing up and relocating. One of the last things I did before departing the East End was to download a Serbian tutorial. I have looked at it exactly zero times. For one thing, I need to be settled, I need a home.

I have been in Key West six weeks and I've switched hotels six times because, well, because I am a fussy bitch – one room too tiny, the next too hot, and onward following the "Princess and the Pea" legacy. Daily I searched the newspapers and Craigslist and plodded around searching for "for rent" signs on houses. One morning, shunting from one rat-bag hotel to the next, I saw a "for rent" sign hanging outside what had once been a pretty Victorian gingerbread, now reduced to a paint-flaking, sagging disaster encircled with a chain link fence. I really didn't want to stop but I didn't like to risk kicking opportunity in the teeth and incurring seven years of bad luck, or whatever the penalty. So I parked in front of a distracted rooster plucking at the dust in the road. I phoned the number on the sign and spoke with a man named Andy. "I own the house but I live in Massachusetts," Andy said. "But there's like a hundred kids in there. Just go knock at the door."

I wanted to hang up on Andy and flee, but then a fetching young man was padlocking a bicycle to the chain-link fence. He was tall, dark and handsome, and I watched his cute ass enter the building.

"It's a bunch of Serbians I've got renting that place," Andy said.

"Did you say Serbs?" I asked, suddenly paying attention.

"Yup! Serbians!" And he snorted.

Phone still pressed against my head, in a couple of strides I was knocking at the front door, where a panel was missing. The door wobbled open, and another, younger, man stood in the hallway. He was in shorts and his hair was tousled and dirty blond, and he was luscious. He wore no shirt, and his smooth tanned torso softened my mood. I hung up the telephone on Andy.

Marko gave me the tour of the gutted wreckage, and I pretended to be interested. When I got to the living room, where a dozen wilting bodies sprawled, I had to ask, "You're all Serbian?" Listlessly they nodded.

"My mother is Princess of Serbia." I declared. They eyed me, skeptically.

Before leaving, I had enlisted the services of beautiful young Marko. He definitely looks like he could take the sting out of studying, especially if I can convince him to keep his shirt off.

Hula Girl

THERE WAS ONE NIGHT I went to a reggae concert on the beach, and in the crowd, there was a girl dancing with a Hula-Hoop. She was young, with long, untidy hair and a long, tight dress and no shoes. She had a way of snaking the hula up above her head, and with her arms stretched she made a tunnel of its descent; she undulated, dancing inside the hoop for maybe a second. Then, with well-practiced hips she caught the blue O and flicked fast side to side, her hard bottom working the toy into a ribbon. Just before the thing reached the ground, she kicked it with her heel and had it back in play. She was desperately sexy.

Her companion – male, rangy and blond, in knee-length shorts and a lot of tattoos – lounged on the sandy dirt leaning on his elbows with his legs out in front of him daintily crossed at the ankle. His attention seemed entirely rapt upon the reggae band. And to be fair, they were good.

I figured this couple must have been together a very long time for him to no longer be mesmerized by his girl's screaming sensuality. Or he was not her boyfriend and, instead, of another persuasion entirely. The only thing I knew for certain was, whoever he was, he could not keep up with her. Few could. No matter, she was a pleasure to behold.

Southernmost

IT WAS A WEDNESDAY evening, a few weeks ago, and I was glumly hibernating in the barren drifts of the East End.

I had been craving change. For one thing, ever since the New Year, I was determined to crack my habit of television time, and it was going to need to be something beyond the glory of shoveling snow.

January was surging unstoppably to the midway mark, that awful moment in man-made time where bright possibilities have begun to dim and taunt.

On the TV, a cheery male apologetically announced an advancing blizzard, and for the millionth time I fired up a travel website. Except that this occasion was different: It was for real, and I bought myself a ticket to Florida. The flight departed in the middle of the following afternoon, but I was ready. After weeks of waffling, my rolling carry-on bag (with coffee-brown zebra motif) was long since packed.

Less than 24 hours later and I was in a rented vanilla Mini Cooper. Something Calypso was coming out of the radio, and I was driving southbound from Fort Lauderdale. Feeling tiny surrounded by a hundred lanes of juggernauts, I was glad to leave the slipknot of Miami and its congestion. An hour or so and the road slimmed to two lanes and bridges connecting ever smaller islands – and ultimately to Key West, where the highway ends in the thronging, narrow streets filled with shops and tourists strolling slowly, touching and fooling with the colorful knickknacks.

I took a room with a porch in the old town – warm rain with hints of jasmine, and mango trees and palm trees and strolling cats, and roving roosters with their warbling lazy calls. Everyone here is from elsewhere, and the first question asked is, "how long are you staying." And when I reply that I traveled here on a one-way ticket, people smile knowingly and mutter, "That's what happened to me years ago."

A pal points out I am following in the footsteps of Ernest Hemingway. Short of producing masterpieces and blasting myself in the head, things might look that way. I'll have to research it, but my guess is Papa did not shoot himself here in the magnificent Keys. This place is too giddily magical to be a tip off for self-destruction. Ergo the only mistake of Papa was to leave.

A local bookstore told me to eff off when I asked after the chances of putting my books on their shelves. Their criterion was that I was not a local. "You gotta be born here, live here or write about here."

In that instant, a decision was forged, "It so happens" – I informed – "I am your newest author in residence. I just moved here."

There are flimsier reasons for relocating a couple thousand miles, but since I've been here, I've forgotten all about television and returned my attention to my true love of reading, everything from Hemingway, to McGuane, to Hiaasen in situ; life doesn't get much better than that.

Conch Fried

IN A BAR, while picking from several plates of ocean dwelling foodstuffs, it was impossible not to notice a couple of hardened drinkers loafing nearby, eyeballing the grub like pelicans. Next upping the nudge to comments, such as, "In my opinion, this place serves the best conch fritters on the whole island," followed by "you gonna eat all that." And since, of course, I was not going to eat all that, I invited the pirate sots to help themselves. They bayed in consternation and then plunged upon the fritters.

Key West

CUSTOMER: (Male, ponytail-ed, with bandy legs and a beer belly, in a sleeveless T-shirt and slept-in, gray shorts) "Have you heard what's happening?"

Cashier: (Female, blonde, weathered, slender, mauve, supple hemp clothing) "You talking about the storm?"

Customer: "It's, like, minus five degrees. There's no reason to rush back."

Cashier: (Smiles.) "I've thought that since the 70's."

Night

KEY WEST, Saturday, midnight, the main street was predictably clogged with revelers.

My attention was splintered by the multitude of merry distractions, and I almost tripped over a month-old chicken. It darted from the sidewalk to the gutter, frenzied, squeaking and lost. Its feathers were tones of gray and muddy browns. With rapid steps it zigzagged, bleating and panicked. I considered repatriating it but I could not see its flock. I pictured picking it up, and then – well, exactly, and then what? I shook off the guilt and walked away.

From an alley came kids screaming and leaping, each equipped with laser swords and walkie-talkies. They barreled by in a cloud of noise and vanished around a corner.

A thin, longhaired man with a top hat, played a guitar and sucked on a harmonica attached to a neck brace.

A suntanned man was using his cell phone to photograph a girl. She stood on the hood of a parked car and pulled up her miniskirt, revealingly. "This is for you," she was saying to him before falling over backwards, to the ground.

Music thumped from everywhere, people strolled about carrying beer in clear plastic beakers.

Standing frozen and alone, on a wood crate, at a busy intersection, a green sequin Elvis impersonator, a study in calm amidst the chaos.

A lithe female in spandex and super-high-heeled shoes swished by, her muscular rump high and solid, her torso tiny, all of her unreal-looking.

It got late, maybe 3:00 in the morning, and the streets were sticky with spilled beer. Herds of young men stumbled with arms around each other's necks, sweating alcohol. Couples argued sloppily in doorways.

Close to home, I saw the little chicken. It laid across the roots of a tree, on its side, crumpled sort of, panting – not the fittest.

Frogs and Such

AFTER A LIFETIME in captivity, one Florida Keys resident's private collection of pond wildlife, frogs and such, turned on each other. These beasts had enjoyed one another's company in a complacent state until Sam, their caretaker, got his plans mixed up, and the daily feeding was overlooked. The animals used to be friends, and now there was tension. They went feral and they did not come back. They began to eat each other. Sam decided to turn the critters loose. "At least they're tough now and can look out for themselves," he reasoned, shooing them down an embankment toward a canal.

In the evening, Sam enjoyed a meditative stroll around the corral island. He absorbed the commingling scents of flowers and dinners cooking and the sounds of music pulsating from low houses. He observed palm trees swaying and greedily inhaled the nourishing Caribbean breeze. Cars passed by slowly enough that the stink of liquor from the passengers hung in the draft.

On his way to the eastern shore, Sam's path took him by a young couple, two fragrant men, their fragrance knitting delicately with the hot night air. He wouldn't mind a friend to walk with, Sam thought, and sniffed at the sweetened air.

Reaching the beach he meandered to the dark end of an unlit pier where wavelets lapped, shattering against the cement. He hadn't seen them until he was almost on them. Two women loomed and asked him to take their photo.

On the return loop from the beach, Sam passed his favorite church – unpainted pine, wide and squat, and a diamond of stained glass on the front of the tower. A cactus grew into the side of a fence. The night-lights translated the driftwood gray to a matte purple hue. Sam discreetly flashed a peace sign and strode by, wishing he wasn't always alone, yet unwilling to abase himself to the company of the women who would have anything to do with him. It had always been this way.

A while later and Sam was a block from home. He was crossing a street when a terrifying rattling noise made him spin around. It sounded like a boat was heading for him. He had only a couple more steps to take before he would be safely across the street. He began turning around as he walked. Swiveling, he noticed it was very dark out. But he could see no headlights. Yet still he heard the noisy rumbling sound. Perhaps a muffler backfiring? He took another step, and he almost made it the other side, when decidedly the sound grew louder.

Sam began jumping now so as to keep his feet from vulnerabilities, hopping sort of and bounding the last step to the sidewalk, leaping over a gaping gutter, painted in red with "drains to ocean." As he leaped through the air to the safety of the sidewalk, he figured out what the dreadful sound was. It was frogs echoing in the gutters.

Save the Whales

I WAS AT THE BEACH when Ella, my favorite do-gooder girlfriend, phoned. "Are you saving the whales?" Ella said. "I'm looking on the Internet, and a couple of miles north you could volunteer to help save a pod of stranded whales."

"I could" – I agreed, as I spread sunblock on me like I was a basting chicken – "but I just plonked down twenty bucks for a chair and an umbrella." We disconnected, and I looked up the whale story. Already there were squadrons of do-gooders clogging the work zone of the rescue effort. Allegedly, the whales were youngsters and they were coughing in small raspy rumbles, blowing bubbles out their spouts. Volunteers hosed the whales and patted them and chattered in understated tones. They gave the whales names, and the volunteers cried as their friends died. Out of 20 whales, five were saved and rolled back into the sea. A week or so later, some of the volunteers came down with whale pneumonia.

From the beach I passed the Key West animal shelter. "Perfection!" I thought and I steered my car from the road and came to a dusty stop in front of a doublewide trailer and a chain-link fence. A sign read "Please do not throw animals over the fence." I entered the trailer to the smell of bleach. A weathered woman with wavy hair like cocker spaniel ears sat at a metal desk.

"I want to walk the dogs, if I may," I said. The woman gave me the once-over and snatched up a three-page questionnaire from a tray. I was appalled by the questions. For example: "Why do you want to walk the dogs? Are you a dog lover? Are you trying to impress someone? Are you trying to impress yourself?"

"Cheeky!" I grumbled under my breath and ticked the box that said I was there for entirely self-serving purposes. To underscore the point, on my way home, I phoned Ella and bragged.

"I hope you feel good." Ella said.

By the time the shelter lady phoned to invite me to orientation I was over my surge of feel-good juice. Life had moved on. I had discovered Eliot and Tango night, and I was hell-bent on introducing one to the other.

At 24, Eliot is already disillusioned. He has a useless college degree, a menial job he despises and a special fondness for cheeseburgers.

144

"A whale of my own to save!" I thought when we met. If I could get him shaking at Tango night, that would be four hours where Eliot was parted from the cheeseburgers. We would dance. Eliot would shed, and I'd get to heaven. Brimming with sanctimony weekly, I texted, "Tango?"

Each week, he replied, "Maybe next week?"

Finally, he responded positively. I was so excited.

But no, he had no desire to attend Tango night. Au contraire, would I like to join him at the all-you-can-eat buffet?

We gorged like Romans.

About the Author

Christina Oxenberg was born, and briefly raised, in New York City. This was followed by prolonged stays in London, then Madrid, then back to New York before returning to London, and so on, until after 14 schools and a multitudinous array of stepparents and their tribes of offspring, a precedent for adventure was set.

Bypassing university, Oxenberg plunged into a whirlpool of random employment, everything from researcher to party organizer to art dealer to burger flipper.

Oxenberg's single true love is writing, and she published her first book, TAXI, a collection of anecdotes, in 1986. Despite the lousy pay, Oxenberg published articles in Allure Magazine, The London Sunday Times Magazine, Tattler, Salon.com, Penthouse and anyone else who would have her.

In 2000, Oxenberg was seduced by the offer of a regular paycheck and she fell down the rabbit-hole world of fine fibers. In the blink of an eye, a decade vanished into an unwieldy wool business. With relief, she returns to the relative calm of writing fiction. Between excursions, she lives in New York City.

Copyright 2011, Leigh Vogel

Made in the USA
Charleston, SC
22 September 2011